Words to Live By

Words to Live By

Using God's Word in Your Everyday Life

EVETTE SMITH-JENKINS

XULON PRESS

Xulon Press
2301 Lucien Way #415
Maitland, FL 32751
407.339.4217
www.xulonpress.com

Unless otherwise indicated, Scripture quotations taken from the King James Reference Bible, copyright 1994 by Zondervan Corporation

Scripture quotations taken from the King James Study Bible, copyright 2002 by Zondervan Corporation

Scripture quotations taken from The Woman's Study Bible, copyright 1995 by Thomas Nelson

Paperback ISBN-13: 978-1-6628-0408-3
Ebook ISBN-13: 978-1-6628-0407-6

John 3:16
"For God so loved the world, that he gave his only begotten Son, that whosoever believeth in him should not perish, but have everlasting life."

Matthew 4:4
Jesus said, "it is written, Man shall not live by bread alone but by every word that proceedth out of the mouth of God."

Galatians 2:20
"I am the crucified with Christ: nevertheless I live; yet not I, but Christ liveth in me: and the life which I now live in the flesh I live by faith of the Son of God, who loved me, and gave himself for me."

Dedicated To

My Children, Family, & Friends

Through the inspiration of the Holy Spirit, I have written this book to let others know God has a word of guidance for whatever they may encounter in this earthly life. And through knowing those words, they can get closer to God in discovering His will and purpose for them.

Contents

Introduction

*In the beginning God created the heavens
and the earth*

Genesis 1:1

*And the Lord God formed man of the dust of
the ground, and breathed into his nostrils the
breath of life and man became a living soul.*

Genesis 2:7

*Jesus said; It is written, that man shall not
live by bread alone, but by every word that
proceedeth out of the mouth of God.*

Matthew 4:4

As human beings, we know that we must eat to nourish our bodies, but our bodies are not the only part of us. The Bible says God made man in His likeness;(Genesis 1:26) God is a spirit so, therefore, we are spirits also. We are all made up of three things: spirit, soul and body. We are spirits with souls that live in bodies. Just as we nourish our bodies with food, we also must nourish our spirits, and our spirits are fed through the Word of God.

There are many individuals who have numerous questions about life and how to find the right answers. In this book I hope to lead you to the biblical scriptures that can bring under-standing and answers to some of your everyday life questions and situations. Sometimes we are in situations where we need to quickly refer to God's Word about how we feel or how to handle a situa-tion or desire. I pray this book brings guidance to you through the Word of God.

My son attend to my words; incline thine ear unto my sayings. Let them not depart from thine eyes; Keep them in the midst of thine heart. For they are life unto those that find them, and health(medicine) to their flesh.
Proverbs 4:20-22

In the Word of God, there are answers to all life's situations and questions, so the decisions we make in life should be based on what God's Word says. We communicate with God through our prayers and in our prayers we should repeat God's written word. God hears our words and knows our hearts and His angels respond to our prayers by hearing God's Word in them. God wants to answer our prayers so we should study His Word to receive it in our hearts..

As children of God, we are to have faith in Him and know that He is there for us. In God's Word, we can find strength, guidance, and wisdom. By trusting in Him and doing His will in our lives, we will have victory!!

Blessings

We all want to be blessed in our lives. As children of God, reading and studying His Word will lead us to what is required to have blessed and fulfilled lives.

> *And it shall come to pass if thou shalt hearken diligently unto the voice of the Lord thy God, to observe and to do all the commandments which I command thee this day, that the Lord will set thee on high above all nations of the earth.*
>
> **Deuteronomy 28:1**

This Scripture states several things – to be diligent unto God; listen to Him and to do His commandments; and that by doing these things, we will be above man and receive the blessings God has in store for you.

> *Blessed is the man that walketh not in the counsel of the ungodly. (2) But his delight is in the word of the Lord; and in God's Word he meditates day and night.*
>
> **Psalm 1:1-2**

We must be consistent in God so He will be consistent with us. God wants to bless us and give us the desires of our hearts, but to receive them, we must do His will in our lives. God didn't create man because He didn't have anything else to do; He created man to have fellowship and companionship with Him. He wants the best for us and to receive His best, we must be diligent in following His Word. No matter what negative situations we face, we should be steadfast in doing God's will, and His will is only found out through studying His Word. We shall receive His blessings and be victorious in life when we follow Him.

For thou Lord, will bless the righteous;
with favour will thou (en)compass him as
with a shield.

Psalm 5:12

The Bible says the Lord will bless the righteous, but what does it mean to be righteous? A righteous person has faith in the Lord and trust and believe in Him with their whole heart. A righteous man or woman lives by God's Word and has faith in His Word. When we live righteously, the Lord God is with us and will protect us from any harm that Satan tries to throw at us.

A faithful man shall abound with blessings:
but he that maketh haste to be rich shall not
be innocent.

Proverbs 28:20

We must know that through faithfulness comes blessings, but for those that do not live by God's Word, there will come judgment for their

3

sins. We shall receive His blessings and be victorious in life when we follow Him.

Comfort

At some time or another we all need to be comforted, whether from losing a loved one, a failed relationship, illness, not succeeding at a goal we set, or when we are being verbally or physically attacked. There are many forms of disappointment we can encounter in our lives, but we must be able to overcome them when we look for comfort. In God's Word, we can find comfort and encouragement to get us through those trying times. God wants us to turn to Him to receive guidance and comfort when we are in trouble or are brokenhearted. Throughout God's Word, we can find many Scriptures that can comfort us as we go through disappointment.

The Lord is my rock, and my fortress, and my deliverer; my God, my strength, in whom I will trust; my buckler, and the horn of my salvation, and my high tower.

Psalm 18:2

Blessed be God, even the Father of our Lord Jesus Christ, the Father of mercies and the God of all comfort; (4) Who comforteth us in all our tribulation that we may be able to comfort them which are in any trouble, by the comfort wherewith we ourselves are comforted of God.

2 Corinthians 1:3-4

God comforts us when we are going through trials. He give us strength and is our shield. We must learn to put our trust in Him to be there for us, no matter what. When we put our trust in God, He will never let us down.

Be careful for nothing [don't let anxiety over take you]; but in everything by prayer

and supplication with thanksgiving let your requests [your worries or concerns] be made known unto God. (7) And the peace of God, which passeth all understanding, shall keep your hearts and minds through Christ Jesus.
Philippians 4:6-7

In 1st King 17, God sent Elijah to the home of a widow who was prepared to die after she and her son had their last meal. Elijah told the her to make him something to eat first. She had to be thinking, *Are you crazy? This is our last bit of food and you want me to give you some first?* Elijah assured her that the Lord would provide and to put her trust in Him. So, the widow did as Elijah asked, and they all ate that day and had plenty of food for many days. We should all be comforted in knowing that God is our salvation.

For his anger endureth but a moment, in his favour is life: weeping may endure for a night but joy cometh in the morning.
Psalm 30:5

This Scripture is saying that when trials occur in life, we must remember that the trials are only for just a moment in time and will not last forever. At the time we are going through the trials of life, it seems like they will never end, but they will. Know that your joy is imminent.

Let the redeemed of the Lord say so, whom he hath redeemed from the hand of the enemy.
Psalm 107:2

Those who believe and trust in God will receive His protection. When the "enemy" comes against us, we don't have to worry because God is there with and for us. He wants us to turn our problems over to Him, because that is how He knows we trust and have faith in Him. As long as we live in this world, we will have trials but we can overcome them when we turn to God and keep our faith in Him.

Jesus said:

> *Verily, verily I say unto you, He that believeth on me, the works that I do shall he do also; and greater works than these shall he do; because I go unto My Father. And whatsoever ye shall ask in my name, that will I do, that the Father may be glorified in the Son. If ye shall ask anything in My name I will do it.*
> ### John 14:12-14

Confidence

Sometimes we need to strengthen our confidence in who we are and what God wants us to be. In God's Word, we can find the words that builds our confidence in ourselves. God wants us to be positive and succeed in all we do. Through His Word, we can conquer negative thoughts and build our confidence. In His Word, we can find encouragement that builds our trust in ourselves and in Him.

Who shall separate us from the love of Christ? Shall tribulation, or distress, or persecution, or famine, or nakedness, or peril, or sword? Nay in all these things we are more than conquerors through Him that loved us.

Romans 8:35, 37

God wants us to know that we are conquerors through all situations. Having faith and trust in Him and knowing that He is always there for us should bring us daily confidence.

Let the redeemed of the Lord say so, whom he hath redeemed from the hand of the enemy.
Psalm 107:2

When we turn to God and put our confidence and trust in Him, He will take care of our enemies and have them at peace with us. *(Heb. 13:6; Prov. 3:25-26; Ps. 23:4).*

And this is the confidence that we have in Him, that if we ask any thing according to His will, he heareth us; and if we know that He hears us, whatsoever we ask, we know that we have the petitions that we desired of Him.
1 John 5:14-15

With strong confidence in the Lord, we are not afraid to ask Him for anything in our prayers.

When we pray, He hears us and wants to bless us with what we need or desire. He can build our confidence to go and get that job we thought we might not be qualified for. He can build our confidence to approach the future love of our lives. He can build our confidence that we will overcome an illness. Having confidence in God builds our confidence in ourselves, and in what we are able to achieve.

> *I called upon the Lord in distress: the Lord answered me, and set me in a large place. The Lord is on my side; I will not fear: What can man do unto me? Therefore, shall I see my desire upon them that hate me. It is better to trust in the Lord, than to put confidence in man.*
>
> ### Psalm 118:5-8

When man lets you down, know that the Lord will never let you down.

Continued

Encouragement

There are many forms of disappointment we can encounter in our lives, but we must be able to overcome them. God's Word has a word of encouragement for us during these disappointments He wants us to trust in Him. He knows when we trust Him, our faith is in Him; and those who believe and trust in God will receive His protection. He wants us to turn our problems over to Him. As long as we live in this world, we will have trials, but we can overcome them when we turn to God for help and keep our faith in Him.

For which cause we faint not, but through our outward man (flesh) perish, yet the inward man (spirit) is renewed day by day. For our light affliction, which is but for a moment, worketh for us a far more exceeding and eternal glory. While we look not at the things, which are seen, but at the things, which are unseen: for the things, which are seen, are temporal, but the things, which are not seen, are eternal.

2 Corinthians 4:16-18

Verily, verily I say unto you, He that believeth on me, the works that I do shall he do also: and greater works than these shall he do; because I go unto My Father. And whatsoever ye shall ask in my name, that will I do, that the Father may be glorified in the Son. If ye shall ask anything in My name I will do it.

John 14:12-14

When we trust and believe in Jesus, we can do all things and even greater things. Jesus did many miracles while He was here on earth. He healed the sick, restored sight to the blind, and even cause a financial issue to be resolved through the mouth of a fish: and He said we could do even more (John 14:12). Wow, just the thought of being able to heal someone or solve financial problems, who doesn't want access to that power? Jesus is our intercessor with God, and whatever we pray and ask in Jesus's name, He will take it to God the Father and it shall be done, as long as it lines up with the Word of God (John 15:7).

> *The thief cometh not, but for to steal and to kill and to destroy: I come that they might have life, and that they might have it more abundantly.*
>
> ### *John 10:10*

In this Scripture, Jesus is saying that Satan wants to bring nothing but heartache in our lives and wants to destroy us. However, Jesus came to save us from Satan, giving us an alternative so that we will have the intended lives and destinies from God. This is because God wants us to live in happiness and harmony.

God wants us to live peaceful lives, even through adversity. He gives us peace and patience to endure what we go through in life.

For ye have need of patience (endurance) that after ye have done the will of God, ye might receive the promise.
Hebrews 10:36

My brethren, count it all joy when ye fall into divers temptations: (3) Knowing this, that the trying of your faith worketh patience. (4) But let patience have her perfect work that ye may be perfect and entire, wanting nothing.
James 1:2-4

Cause me to hear thy lovingkindness in the morning: for in thee I do trust: cause me to know the way wherein I should walk; for I lift up my soul unto thee.
Psalm 143:8

Be encouraged, knowing that through God, all wonderful things in life are possible, as long as we trust Him and do His will in our lives.

Faith

What is faith? According to Hebrews 11:1, *"Now faith is the substance of things hoped for, the evidence of things not seen."* This means even though you don't see something manifested yet, you know it will happen in faith.

> But without faith it is impossible to please God: for he that cometh to God must believe that He is, and that He is a rewarder of them that diligently seek Him.
>
> **Hebrews 11:6**

Not having faith in God means you don't believe who He is or trust in Him. God can't bring you out of tribulation when you don't have faith in who He is, because having faith in God means knowing He can bring you out of bad situations.

21

Having faith in God means He can cause you to have favor with man. Having faith in God will bring victory in your life.

> *Even so faith if it hath not works is dead being alone.*
>
> **James 2:17**

> *For as the body without the spirit is dead, so faith without works is dead.*
>
> **James 2:26**

These verses are saying we must put action into our faith in order for our faith to work. In Matthew 9:20-21, there was a woman with an ailment that she suffered with for twelve years and all the doctors she had seen could not heal her. When she heard of Jesus and all the miracles He had done, she knew she had to see Him. Her faith in Jesus made her push her way through the crowd of people waiting to see Jesus just to touch Him. She knew that if she just touched His garment, she knew she would be healed. In Matthew 9:22, Jesus tells the woman *"...Daughter be of good comfort thy faith hath made thee whole."*

For we walk by faith and not by sight.
2 Corinthians 5:7

If you need healing, you should believe God for your healing, but also find the Scriptures in God's Word that relates to being healed and read them daily until your healing is manifested. Receiving God's best in life is based on your faith in Him. Reading His Word alone will not bring what you need unless you have faith God will do what His Word says.

Having faith in God is not all we need to get the results we want; we must also put action into our faith. If someone is looking for a job, it's not going to come to him or her out of the blue. The person has to prepare for the job he/she wants. The person has to know what it takes to do the job, and then go out and submit applications to get the process in motion, putting his/her faith in God that the person will get hired.

...if ye have faith as a grain of a mustard seed, ye shall say unto this mountain, remove hence to yonder place; and it shall remove; and nothing shall be impossible unto you.

Matthew 17:20

In this verse, Jesus was telling the disciples that it only takes a little bit of faith to change a situation. But you have to believe in your heart and have faith that God will make it happen.

When we accept Jesus as Lord of our lives, we must also put our faith in Him. Jesus came so that we would have more abundant lives. We must trust Him and show our faith and trust by leaning on Him; and know that following God's Word and will, our prayers will be answered.

Even though we have never seen Jesus, we have faith in knowing He is our Savior and through Him, our sins can be forgiven. Through repentance and asking for forgiveness, our sins are erased.

Favor

What does it mean to have favor? Favor is an unexplained blessing in your life, which can be obtained by believing and trusting in God. When you depend on God and call on Him for answers, doors will open in the natural, because God can cause supernatural results. When you think something is impossible in a situation, God can make it happen. When we live as God wants us to, we can ask Him for something specific and know from looking at the situation, it is not possible to receive unless something supernatural did happen.

So shall thou find favour and good understanding in the sight of God and man?
Proverbs 3:4

For thou Lord, wilt bless the righteous with favour wilt thou compass him as with a shield.
Psalms 5:12

For the Lord God is a sun and shield: The Lord will give grace and glory, no good thing will He withhold from them that walk uprightly.
Psalms 84:11

A good name is rather to be chosen than great riches, and loving favour rather than silver and gold.
Proverbs 22:1

A good man obtaineth favour of the Lord, but a man of wicked devices will be condemned.
Proverbs 12:2

These Scriptures let us know that favor from God is a gift to the righteous, and is more precious than anything that man can give us. With favor from God, we can overcome all odds. Favor from

God is much more precious than riches and gold from man, because through God's favor, we obtain all we need and more.

Fear

According to God's Word, He has not given us a spirit of fear (2 Timothy 1:7). When negative things occur in our lives, we should not be afraid because God is our provider and protector. Through all the fears and worries of this world (sickness, death, financial problems, etc.), God is there for us when we turn to Him.

For God hath not given us the spirit of fear; but of power, and love, and of a sound-mind(self-control).
2 Timothy 1:7

Fear not; for I am with thee: Be not dismayed; for I am thy God: I will strengthen thee; yea, I will help thee; yea I will uphold thee with the right hand of my righteousness.
Isaiah 41:10

When we put our trust in God, we can overcome all of this world's troubles. God does not want us to live in fear, because when we live in fear, that means we are not putting our trust in Him.

Ye are of God, little children and have overcome them: because greater is He (Holy Spirit) that is in you than he (Satan) that is in the world.

1 John 4:4

When we accepted Jesus as Savior of our lives, He became part of who we are. The Holy Spirit dwells in us and through the power of the Holy Spirit, we have the power of God in us.

Forgiveness

We must forgive those who have wronged us, for if we do not forgive others, how can God forgive us of our sins? No matter how hurt we are from the wrong someone has done to us, it is God's will that we forgive him or her. When we go to God, asking for forgiveness, we must also think from our hearts and ask ourselves have we forgiven those who have hurt us.

> Judge not, and ye shall not be judged: condemn not, and ye shall not be condemned: forgive, and ye shall be forgiven:
> **Luke 6:37**

We are not to judge others but to forgive them. God will judge them in eternity.

Wherefore I say unto thee, her sins which are many, are forgiven; for she loved much: but to whom little is forgiven, the same loveth little.
Luke 7:47

The scripture above is referring to when Jesus knew what Simon was thinking when Simon saw a sinner woman washing Jesus's feet and anointed them with a fragrant oil. Simon thought if Jesus was a true prophet, he would know that she was a sinner and would not let her touch him. The woman was showing her love for Jesus by washing His feet and Jesus tells Simon that by the woman showing her love for Him her sins were forgiven, but those that show little love will receive little forgiveness from God.

And be ye kind one to another, tenderhearted, forgiving one another, even as God for Christ's sake hath forgiven you.
Ephesians 4:32

For if ye forgive men their trespasses, your heavenly Father will also forgive you; (15) But if ye forgive not men their trespasses, neither will your Father forgive your trespasses.
Matthew 6:14-15

And when ye stand praying, forgive, if ye have ought against any: that your Father also which is in heaven, may forgive you your trespasses. (26) But if you do not forgive, neither will you Father which is in heaven forgive your trespasses.
Mark 11:25-26

In each of these Scriptures, it says we are to forgive to be forgiven. Not forgiving others can hinder healing from manifesting in your body. Unforgiveness is against what God's Word says. We are to forgive one another just as God forgives us of our sins. (Colossians 3:13)

Grace

Grace is a gift from God, and there is nothing we could have done in life that allows us to receive God's grace, except to accept Jesus as our Savior over our lives. Grace is unearned favor from God.

For by grace are ye saved through faith and that not of yourselves it is the gift of God: Not of works, lest any man should boast.
Ephesians 2:8-9

For the Lord God is a sun and shield: The Lord will give grace and glory: no good thing will be withheld from them that walk uprightly.
Psalm 84:11

For the law was given by Moses, but grace and truth came by Jesus Christ.

John 1:17

Grace is a gift we receive without giving, and mercy is what we receive even though we don't deserve it. As Christians with faith in God and believers of Jesus Christ, God gives us grace and mercy no matter what we have done, as long as we call upon Him and ask for forgiveness when we have sinned.

For sin shall not have dominion over you: for ye are not under the law, but under grace.
Romans 6:14

Let us therefore come boldly unto the throne of grace that we may obtain mercy and find grace to help in time of need.
Hebrews 4:16

Healing

We all want to be healthy. When sickness comes upon our bodies, and after we receive a diagnosis from the doctor then we go to God in prayer. We are to pray to God for healing and go to His Word that says we are healed, meditating on God's Word over our bodies until our healing has manifested. Through our faith and trust in God know that our healing is imminent.

For I will restore health unto thee and I will heal thee of thy wounds saith the Lord...
Jeremiah 30:17

God has a purpose for us, and to do His will effectively, He knows we have to be healthy. When we live as God desires and pray that we are healed,

God will hear our prayers and our healing will be manifested. Those who die doing Gods will in their lives may not receive healing because they may have finished their assignment that God had for them, or have hidden sin or unforgiveness in their life.

> *But He was wounded for our transgressions, He was bruised for our iniquities: the chastisement of our peace was upon Him and with His stripes we are healed.*
>
> **Isaiah 53:5**

Jesus came so that we would be restored to God and to do His will in our lives.

The Lord Jesus Christ sacrificed His life so we would prosper in all areas of our lives, which includes good health. Jesus came to give us abundant life, and to have power over sickness and disease, and to know that we are to give no place for either in our lives.

God wants us to have faith in Him. He knows our needs, which include healing in our bodies when we are sick. When we live as God desires and pray for our healing in Jesus's name, God will hear us and bring our prayers into existence. We must believe and have strong faith that God has healed us even before our healing has manifested.

And His name through faith in his name hath made this man strong, whom ye see and know: yea, the faith, which is by him, hath given him this perfect soundness in the presence of you all.

Acts 3:16

After Jesus was resurrected and ascended to heaven, Peter and John healed the sick through their faith and the power of Jesus's name. Through this same type of faith, we can heal others and ourselves. We must remember, though, that un-forgiveness toward others can also hinder our healing. When we hold unforgiveness towards anyone God will not hear our prayers concerning healing and prayers for other things (Isaiah 59:2). Unforgiveness affects our emotional and spiritual health along with our physical health. Holding unforgiveness in your heart is like holding sickness in your body.

Love

We all want to have love in our lives, love comes in many forms and has many definitions. In Greek, there are different words for each type of love: love for your family is called storge (natural affection) love; love for your friends is called philia (loyalty) love; love for your spouse is Eros (passionate) love; and love for God is agape (unconditional) love.

However, our love for family and friends does not compare to the love God has for us, as He has unconditional love for us. Through God's love for us, He gave the ultimate sacrifice for us — His Son Jesus.

For God so loved the world that He gave His only begotten Son, that whosoever believeth

*in Him should not perish but have ever-
lasting life.*

John 3:16

*Beloved let us love one another: for love is of
God; and everyone that loveth is born of God
and knoweth God.*

1 John 4:7

God is love and He loves us all no matter what,
because He wants the best for us. God's ultimate
sacrifice was so we who accept Him would have
eternal life with Him. That is why He sent Jesus
so that we can be redeemed of our sins. We must
also love each other and want what is best for each
other, even loving our enemies.

*But I say unto you, love your enemies, bless
them that curse you, do good to them that
hate you and pray for them which despite-
fully use you and persecute you.*

Matthew 5:44

This is my commandment, that ye love one another as I have loved you.
John 15:12

Jesus gave us this new commandment when He walked the earth and through obedience of His commandment, we are also keeping the commandments that God gave Moses. This is because through love for one another, we would not hurt one another or misuse each other. God wants us to love others as we would love ourselves. We don't want to hurt ourselves so we should not want to hurt others.

If ye keep my commandments ye shall abide in my love; even as I have kept my Father's commandments and abide in His love.
John 15:10

Obedience

We must obey God and do His will in our lives in order to be able to receive the blessings He has for us and achieve the prosperity He wants for us. Living in the will of God allows us to receive His grace and mercy when we do mess up in life.

Doing God's will and obeying His Word brings blessings not only to the one obeying Him, but also to those around them. Most of the time we think about what we do in life and about how it will affect us, but our obedience to God impacts not only us but also those we love. If God revealed an assignment to you and you have not done it, by not doing it, you may have caused others to miss out on something that should have happened in their lives. Your lack of obedience may cause others not to receive or hear what they should from God, since you failed to do the will of God.

God has not only given us commandments to live by, but He has given us assignments that we must follow. We all have God-given gifts and assignments in life: preacher, teacher, prophet, or helper. It is up to us to find out our God-given missions in life. Through prayer and meditation in God's Word, He will reveal our assignments and then we must be obedient in doing them.

And being made perfect, he became the author of eternal salvation unto them that obey him;
Hebrews 5:9

Jesus was obedient to God by fulfilling the will God had for Him in His life and through His obedience, we now have access to have eternal life with Him and God (Matt. 26:39; Mark 14: 35-36; Luke 22:42-44). The Word says obedience is better than sacrifice (1 Sam. 15:22).

Obey them that have rule over you, and submit yourselves: for they watch for your souls, as they that must give account, that they may do it with joy, and not with grief: for that is unprofitable for you.

Hebrews 13:17

Just as Jesus obeyed God the Father, it is a blessing for children to obey their parents. When we obey and honor our parents, we will have long life.

Children, obey your parents in the Lord: for this is right. Honour thy father and mother; (which is the first commandment with promise;) That it may be well with thee, and thou mayest live long on the earth.

Ephesians 6:1-3

Peace

We all want peace in our lives, and depending on God brings us that peace. In times of pain and sorrow, we look for peace and contentment that bring us comfort in those trying times and situations.

We can find peace when we're told our jobs are being terminated because God's Word says:

Peace I leave with you, my peace I give unto you: not as the world giveth, give I unto you. Let not your heart be troubled, neither let it be afraid.

John 14:27

We can find peace when a decision has to be made and when we look to God for direction. We are to meditate on His Word that can bring revelation to us from the Holy Spirit.

To obtain access to God's peace, we must study and meditate on His Word and get His Word in our hearts so when we need to call on it, the answer will come to our remembrance. The Holy Spirit will bring you the answer you are searching for when the Word is in your heart.

> *Be careful for nothing; but in everything by prayer and supplication with thanksgiving let your requests be made know unto God. (7) And the peace of God, which passeth all understanding, shall keep your hearts and minds through Christ Jesus.*
>
> ***Philippians 4:6-7***

Peace is the absence of fear. We can find peace when the doctor tells us of a sickness or disease we have, for we know that Jesus suffered for us. He bore our sickness, healed us of all diseases, and by His stripes we were healed(1 Peter 2:24). This means we are already healed. So, we should find peace in knowing this by claiming that "I am healed in Jesus's name."

> .... brethren, whatsoever things are true, whatsoever things are honest, whatsoever things are just, whatsoever things are pure, whatsoever things are lovely, whatsoever things are of good report; if there be any virtue, and if there be any praise, think on these things. (9) Those things, which ye have both learned, and received, and heard, and seen in me, do: and the God of peace shall be with you.
>
> **Philippians 4:8-9**

In this Scripture, Paul was telling the people of Philippi to think on good things and rejoice in the Lord, knowing that He will take care of any trying times they may be going through, and so should we.

Praise

When praises go up, blessings come down; this is not just a cliché phrase but the truth. When we have faith in God and believe in our hearts(truly trusting Him), then we should start praising God for victory in every situation good or bad. Know that you have the victory through Him who loves you.

Make a joyful noise unto the Lord, all ye lands. (2) Serve the Lord with gladness: Come before His presence with singing. (3) Know ye that the lord He is God; It is He that hath made us, and not we ourselves; We are his people, and the sheep of his pasture. (4) Enter into his gates with thanksgiving, and into his courts with praise: Be thankful unto him, and bless his name. (5) For the Lord is good; his mercy is everlasting; And his truth endureth to all generations.

Psalm 100: 1-5

Because thy loving-kindness is better than life, My lips shall praise thee. (4) Thus will I bless thee while I live: I will lift up my hands in thy name. (5) My soul shall be satisfied as with marrow and fatness; And my mouth shall praise thee with joyful lips: (6) When I remember thee upon my bed, and meditate on thee in the night watches. (7) Because thou hast been my help, therefore in the shadow of thy wings will I rejoice.

Psalm 63: 3-7

When God hears our praises and thanks to Him, He knows we are trusting in Him. God loves us and wants us to be victorious in life.

Prayer

P rayer is our direct communication with God, for God hears the prayers of the righteous. Who are the righteous? The righteous are those who have accepted Jesus Christ as their Savior and believe in Him.

> ...The effectual fervent prayer of a righteous man availeth much.
>
> **James 5:16**

Without believing in Jesus, our prayers fall on deaf ears. Jesus is our intercessor with God, so if you don't believe in Him, God does not get your prayers.

> Who is he that condemneth? It is Christ that died, yea rather, that is risen again, who

is even at the right hand of God, who also maketh intercession for us.

Romans 8:34

When we are not sure what to pray for in a certain situation, we should pray in the Holy Spirit.

Likewise the Spirit also helpth our infirmities: for we know not what we should pray for as we ought: but the Spirit itself maketh intercession for us with groaning's which cannot be uttered.

Romans 8:26

If you are not sure how to pray, Jesus gives a model prayer in Matthew 6:9-13. Also, in our prayer time, it is not just to ask God for what we need and want, but also to ask Him what does He want us to do. Ask the Lord, "What would you have me to do today?" and He will speak to you with a thought in your mind. You will know it is from God, because it will line up with His Word.

*And all things, whatsoever ye shall ask in
prayer, believing ye shall receive.*

Matthew 21:22

Prayer is powerful. Continuing in prayer and
believing He will answer our prayers brings results.
God wants to bless us and give us what we need
and desire.

Purity

Being holy and pure is part of gaining access to God's blessings in your life. In the dictionary, it states the meaning of purity as: the state of being pure, to be free from guilt or moral blemish[1]. The Bible references purity as having a pure heart (godly character), having a loving spirit, and keeping oneself clean from sin)1 Timothy 5:22).

Wherewithal shall a young man cleanse his way? By taking heed thereto according to thy word. (10) With my whole heart have I sought thee; O let me not wander from thy commandments. (11) Thy word have I hid in mine heart that I might not sin against thee.

Psalm 119:9-11

---

[1] Merriam-Webster dictionary

59

Let no man despise thy youth; but be thou an example of the believers, in word, in conversation, in charity, in spirit, in faith in purity.
1 Timothy 4:12

Lay hands suddenly on no man, neither be partaker of other men's sins: keep thyself pure.
1 Timothy 5:22

We can have a pure body and mind by living according to the Word of God.
Draw nigh to God, and he will draw nigh to you. Cleanse your hands, ye sinners; and purify your hearts, ye double minded.
James 4:8

How much more shall the blood of Christ, who through the eternal spirit offered himself without spot to God, purge(purify) your conscience from dead works to serve the living God.

Hebrews 9:14

But if we walk in the light, as he is in the light, we have fellowship one with another; and the blood of Jesus Christ his son cleanseth (purifies) us from all sin. (8) If we say that we have no sin, we deceive ourselves, and the truth is not in us. (9) If we confess our sins, he is faithful and just to forgive us our sins, and to cleanse us from all unrighteousness.

1 John 1:7-9

Relationships

Everyone wants peaceful relationships with all the people they encounter in life: spouse, family, friends, and co-workers. God's Word says to love your neighbor as yourself (Matt. 22:39). If we love everyone as much as we love ourselves, the world would be a better place.

We can find guidance through God's Word on how we should handle the different types of relationships in our lives.

Spouse – *Wives, submit yourselves unto your own husbands as unto the Lord. (23) For the husband is the head of the wife, even as Christ is the head of the church: and he is the savior of the body. (24) Therefore, as the church is subject unto Christ, so let the wives be to their own husbands in everything. (25)*

Husbands, love your wives, even as Christ also loved the church, and gave himself for it; (28) so ought men to love their wives as their own bodies. He that loveth his wife loveth himself.

Ephesians 5:22-25, 28

Husbands, love your wives, and be not bitter against them.

Colossians 3:19

Children – *And all thy children shall be taught of the Lord; And great shall be the peace of thy children.*

Isaiah 54:13

Children, obey your parents in all things; for this is well pleasing unto the Lord. (21) Fathers, provoke not your children to anger, lest they be discouraged.

Colossians 3:20-21

Family – *Trust in the Lord with all thine heart; and lean not unto thine own understanding*
(6) In all thy ways acknowledge him, and he shall direct thy paths.

Proverbs 3:5-6

Train up a child in the way he should go: and when he is old, he will not depart from it.

Proverbs 22:6

I (God) call heaven and earth to record this day against you, that I have set before you life and death, blessing and cursing: therefore choose life, that both thou and thy seed may live.

Deuteronomy 30:19

Friends – *A man that hath friends must shew himself friendly: and there is a friend that sticketh closer than a brother.*

Proverbs 18:24

Make no friendship with an angry man.
Proverbs 22:24

Greater Love hath no man than this, that a man lay down his life for his friend.
John 15:13

And the scripture was fulfilled which saith, Abraham believed God, and it was imputed unto him for righteousness; and he was called the Friend of God.
James 2:23

God will direct favor in our lives with our friends, co-workers, and those in authority over us.

For thou, Lord wilt bless the righteous; with favour wilt thou compass him as with a shield.
Psalm 5:12

Salvation

There are many people who want to know why we need salvation. We need salvation because Adam and Eve disobeyed God by eating from the Tree of Knowledge of Good and Evil, which God had told them not to. Eating from this tree was direct disobedience of God, which caused sin to enter into this world; thereby, anyone born into this world is a sinner (Rom. 5:12). When Adam sinned, he gave this world over to Satan.

God gave us a way to regain our right standing with Him, which was by Him sending His Son Jesus into this world. Jesus came to redeem our sins for us. He came to die and deal with Satan, overcoming Satan in hell and was resurrected from death so we could have eternal life with Him and God (John 3:16).

You can only receive salvation by accepting Jesus Christ as your Savior.

Be it known unto you all, and to all the people of Israel, that by the name of Jesus Christ of Nazareth, whom ye crucified, whom God raised from the dead, even by him doth this man stand here before you whole. (12) Neither is there salvation in any other for there is none other name under heaven given among men, whereby we must be saved.

Acts 4:10, 12

You can receive salvation by confessing with your month that you believe Jesus Christ is the Son of God, and that He died and rose again so we could have eternal life with Him and God.

... if thou shalt confess with thy mouth the Lord Jesus, and shalt believe in thine heart that God hath raised him form the dead, thou shalt be saved. (10) For with the heart

man believeth unto righteousness; and with
the mouth confession is made unto salvation.
Romans 10:9-10

When you want to accept Jesus as Lord of
your life, you must say the prayer of salvation. This
prayer is acknowledging Jesus for who He is and
that you believe He died for you to remove your
sins, so your spirit will have eternal life with Him
and God the Father. (Salvation Prayer on page 83.)

Salvation is a gift from God through His grace
and mercy (Eph. 2:8-9). There is nothing we need
to do other than accept Jesus into our lives (John
1:12) to receive salvation.

Wisdom

The Word of God gives us wisdom, providing us with information in all areas of our lives. It gives us knowledge on how we should handle all situations as God would handle them. When we ask God for the wisdom on how to handle a situation, He will give it to us. God will direct us through His Word or the Holy Spirit, which will reveal things to us that will always line up with the Word of God.

My son, if thou wilt receive my words and hide my commandments with thee (2) So that thou incline thine ear unto wisdom, and apply thine heart to understanding; (3) Yea, if thou criest after knowledge, and liftest up thy voice for understanding; (4) If Thou seekest her as silver and searchest for her as for hid treasures; (5) Then shall thou understand the fear of the Lord, and find the knowledge of God. (6) For the Lord giveth wisdom: Out of his mouth cometh knowledge and understanding.

Proverbs 2:1-6

The fear of the Lord is the beginning wisdom: A good understanding have all they that do his commandments: His praise endureth forever.
Psalm 111:10

If any of you lack wisdom, let him ask of God that giveth to all men liberally, and upbraideth not: and it shall be given him.
James 1:5

Wisdom is the principal thing, therefore get wisdom: and with all they getting get understanding. (8) Exalt her, and she shall promote thee: She shall bring thee to honour, when thou dost embrace her. (9) She shall *give thine head an ornament of grace: A crown of glory shall he deliver to thee.*

Proverbs 4:7-9

... the wisdom that is from above is first pure, then peaceable, gentle and easy to be intreated, full of mercy and good fruits, without partiality, and without hypocrisy.

James 3:17

These Scriptures let us know wisdom is received through God and His Word, which means we must study His Word to receive a complete understanding of God and to be able to gain the wisdom He has for us. The book of Proverbs gives us guidance in life: how we should live daily; who we should befriend in life; how we should guide our children; how our children are to treat their parents; how we should handle situations and so on. Reading the book of Proverbs would be very helpful throughout life. Living as God would have us live is wisdom.

73

Spiritual Eternity

Where will you spend eternity? Heaven or hell? With Jesus or Satan?

Just as there are stars in the sky, there is also a heaven and a hell. If you died today, do you know where your spiritual eternity would be? We are made up of three things: soul, body, and spirit. We have a soul that is made up of our mind, will and emotions. We have a physical body and we have a spirit. This is also stated as, we are a spirit that has a soul that lives in a body.

If you are unsure of your eternity, there is one way to ensure you spend it with God. You must repent of your sins and ask God to forgive you for your sins. When you ask God for forgiveness, God will no longer remember your sins(Hebrews 10:16-18). Once we ask for forgiveness, we must say the Prayer of Salvation (shown on page 83).

Receiving Salvation

If you have read this book and you have not accepted Jesus as your Savior, you can get in right standing with God by saying the "Prayer of Salvation" on page 83.

Or, maybe you once accepted Jesus as Lord of your life, but you have now fallen away from Him and you are out of fellowship with God. You can give your life back to God by saying the "Prayer of Rededication" on page 85.

God's Word says:

> ... if thou shalt confess with thy mouth the Lord Jesus, and shalt believe in thine heart that God hath raised him from the dead, thou shalt be saved.
>
> ***Romans 10:9***

The Rapture

The Rapture is not the "Second coming of Jesus" to earth; it is when Jesus comes to take those to heaven that believe in Him and do God's will. During the Rapture, the dead in Christ will be taken up first and then the Church (the living in Christ). Are you living for Christ? Are you doing God's will in your life? Are you bringing others to Christ? If you answered no to any of these questions, you need to get right with God so you will be part of the Rapture of Christ.

> But I would not have you to be ignorant, brethren, concerning them which are asleep (dead in Christ), that ye sorrow not, even as others which have no hope. (14) For if we believe that Jesus died and rose again, even so them also which sleep in Jesus will God bring

with him. (15) For this we say unto you by the word of the Lord, that we, which are alive and remain unto the coming of the Lord shall not prevent them which are sleep. (16) For the Lord himself shall descend from heaven with a shout, with the voice of the archangel, and with the trump of God: and the dead in Christ shall rise first: (17) Then we which are alive and remain shall be caught up together with them in the clouds, to meet the Lord in the air: and so shall we ever with the Lord.

1 Thessalonians 4:13-17

The Tribulation

The Tribulation (the wrath of God) is what will happen after the Rapture has occurred. The anti-Christ (who signs a declaration of peace) will be revealed and will rule the earth. The living on earth will go through much pain and sorrow during this time.

> *And then shall the Wicked be revealed, whom the Lord shall consume with the spirit of his mouth, and shall destroy with the brightness of his coming: (9) Even him, whose coming is after the working of Satan with all power and signs and lying wonders. (10) And with all deceivableness of unrighteousness in them that perish; because they received not the love of the truth that they might be saved.*
> **2 Thessalonians 2:8-10**

Prayer of Salvation

I believe that Jesus is the Son of God. I believe that He died for me on Calvary(the place outside of Jerusalem where Jesus was crucified). I believe that He rose from the dead and now is alive. Dear Jesus, come into my life now. Come into my heart now. I accept You as my Lord and Savior, and I am now born again.

In Jesus's name, Amen.

Prayer of Rededication

Lord, I confess my sins (state your sins) and I come back to You asking for forgiveness so I may be in right standing again with You, Lord. I thank you for Your Son Jesus Christ, who came that we receive redemption for our sins. Lord, thank you for Your grace and mercy. Amen!

If we confess our sins, He is faithful and just to forgive us our sins, and to cleanse us from all unrighteousness.

1 John 1:9

Daily Commitment Prayer

Father in heaven, I come to You in Jesus Christ's holy name. I renew my spirit in You Lord. I commit to obey Your Word and do Your will daily, and to be a living sacrifice for You. I give my life to You, Lord, now and for eternity. I ask You, Lord, to bind all that I am and to be all that You are, in Christ Jesus. Amen!

Notes

_____

_____

_____

_____

_____

_____

_____

_____

_____

_____

_____

_____

_____

_____

_____

_____

_____

_____

_____

_____

_____

_____

_____

_____

CPSIA information can be obtained
at www.ICGtesting.com
Printed in the USA
BVHW041741240321
603339BV00005B/522

9 781662 804083